WILD HORSES OF SABLE ISLAND

By Zoe Lucas

An OWL Book
Published by Greey de Pencier Books, 1981
Toronto, Canada
© Zoe Lucas
ISBN 0-919872-73-5
Printed in Canada

Out in the Atlantic Ocean, off the coast of Nova Scotia, there is a lonely place called Sable Island. The island is not much more than a sand bar. There are no trees, only sand dunes covered with beach grasses, with a few fresh water ponds and cranberry bogs in the hollows.

In times past there had been hundreds of shipwrecks along the island's windswept and foggy shores. And that may be how wild horses came to be there. Perhaps many years ago a few horses escaped the sinking ships and the stormy sea, and managed to reach the beaches. Now about thirty to forty small family herds make Sable Island their home.

A young stallion called Seafire is one of these island horses. He is the colour of the sun rising over the sea and has a spirit to match.

Until last spring, Seafire spent most of his time alone. He watched the other horses from a distance and wandered the dunes learning about the island. He explored the hills and hollows, and discovered the fresh water ponds. He ambled about, ankle deep amongst the water-weeds, peacefully nibbling the new shoots. But as the days grew longer and warmer, Seafire became more interested in the other horses and began to follow the small groups closely.

Then with mid-summer a whole new kind of life began for the young stallion. Several mares joined him, and so Seafire had a family herd of his own.

The small herd spent the rest of the summer together, enjoying the warm days and the rich green plants. One of the mares, who was older and more experienced, led the group from place to place, to wherever she recalled that good food or shelter could be found.

As for Seafire, his carefree days of wandering over the dunes and dozing in the summer sunshine were over. It was up to him to keep the herd together. While the senior mare led the group into pastures of beach grass, he followed along watchfully, snatching mouthfuls of grass as he looked out for intruders. More often than not there would be another stallion ready to challenge Seafire and try to steal his mares away.

One stallion, older and bigger than Seafire, was a particular nuisance. His name was Northwind. Whenever Northwind appeared, Seafire would dash over to meet him and the two horses would dance about each other, smell each other, and push and shove. If that didn't sort out who was who a kick or two would settle the matter. But peace would only last a while. Each time Seafire just managed to drive Northwind away. But Northwind returned again and again throughout the summer to bother Seafire and the mares.

As winter approached, the lush green pastures turned to fields of poor hay and straw. Rainstorms came with the cold northwest winds, and day after day Seafire's family became more wet and miserable. Led by the senior mare, the herd went from here to there looking for better food and places to hide from the wild sea winds.

The horses found some protection in the hollows between the sand dunes. Standing close to the sandy walls, they would wait for the worst of the storms to pass. As the horses of Sable Island did every winter, Seafire and the mares had grown thick, woolly coats to keep themselves a little warmer, but even so, they were very uncomfortable.

Then the snow came, and along with it freezing rain.
Blowing sand and snow covered the horses and stung their

eyes. The senior mare huddled the herd close together for warmth. It was the best they could do.

The horses were not the only animals on the dunes. For
centuries big grey seals had been coming to Sable Island,
and they came this winter as always. Thousands of seals
came out of the ocean, hauling themselves across the
beaches and onto the dunes where they would give birth to

their pups. Because the seals had a thick layer of blubber
beneath their skins, the cold didn't bother them. Nor did
the rain, snow and ice. So while the horses shivered
miserably, the seals sleepily waited for their pups to be
born.

When the seal pups arrived, they, like their parents, were unconcerned about the winter weather. They grew full and fat on rich seal milk and lay about like round, furry bundles. With backs to the wind, flippers clasped over their stomachs and eyes squeezed shut, they slept until the time came for them to go to the sea. For the horses there

was no such peace. This was one of the hardest Sable Island winters in many years. The beach grass made such poor hay that to have enough energy to keep warm, the horses had to depend upon the reserved strength they had built up over the summer. It was a very long winter, and those that were in poorest condition could not survive.

Finally spring arrived. Seafire and the mares were thin and weak, and very tired. But they were all alive!

Whenever the sun shone they would stand about happily soaking up the warmth. And as the sun shone more often, they began to lose their woolly coats. The grasses grew slowly at first, but eventually came up tall and green, and there were fine pastures once again.

But Seafire's troubles were not over yet. So many horses had died over the winter that there were a number of stallions on the island without herds, and many of the younger horses did not have experienced mares to guide them. What an uproar this caused on Sable Island! Horses galloped about, chasing and fighting each other. There were many challenges and threats and very few agreements. Seafire was kept so busy guarding his mares he got very little rest.

But that wasn't all the excitement. One of the mares in Seafire's herd had a foal, a little fellow with bright eyes and a sandy coloured nose. Because of the hard winter, he was one of the few horses born on Sable Island that spring.

At first he stayed close to the mares while he practised balancing on his thin and wobbly legs. But it wasn't long before he was leaping and running about, learning the ways of the herd and discovering the sweet taste of the waterweeds.

Then, one day, Northwind, who hadn't been seen since the summer before, arrived as big and bold as ever. Seafire dashed to meet him and keep him away from the herd. Northwind pranced and pushed, Seafire reared and threatened. But Seafire was no longer the young and inexperienced stallion of the previous summer. Suddenly the fight seemed too much for Northwind and off he galloped, over the dunes and away!

Northwind never came back to bother Seafire again. Although he would be challenged by many other stallions in the future, Seafire was able to protect his family. He knew it, Northwind knew it, and the mares were sure of it!

As for the foal, he spent a warm and wonderful summer. He grew and played and learned as his father had done, and perhaps some day he too would be galloping the dunes, exploring the island—and ready for a herd of his own.

Canadian Cataloguing in Publication Data

Lucas, Zoe, 1950-
Wild horses of Sable Island

(An Owl true adventure book)

ISBN 0-919872-73-5

1. Wild horses—Nova Scotia—Sable Island—Juvenile
literature. I. Title. II. Series.

SF284.S22L82   j599.72'5   C81-094933-4